BRONTË RELICS

A COLLECTION HISTORY

Ann Dinsdale, Sarah Laycock and Julie Akhurst

The Brontë Society

ISBN: 978-1-903007-15-0

Designed by Stubbs Design

Printed by The Print Academy (Yorkshire) Limited

Introduction

WRITERS' LIVES TEND to be as fascinating to us as their fictions, even when there is relatively little biographical information available. In fact, the less we know the more fascinated we become. Certainly, the Brontës have exerted an extraordinarily powerful hold over our collective imagination for more than 150 years now. Generations of readers, writers, and artists have been absorbed and inspired by them and they have permeated our cultural landscape, at every level. We are the Brontës.

The Brontës' cultural pervasiveness is largely explained by the power of the stories they created, but the story of the Brontës' own lives has been, and continues to be, equally compelling. It is easy to understand why, with so many irresistible components: the wild moorland landscape surrounding Haworth; the spectre of early family bereavement; the intense imaginative worlds of childhood; the remarkable literary achievement of three sisters all writing great English novels under one roof; the precociously talented but fatally flawed brother; and of course the 'tragic' early deaths.

It was Charlotte Brontë's friend, the novelist Mrs Gaskell, who wrote the first Brontë biography in 1857, within two years of Charlotte's death. Her *The Life of Charlotte Brontë*, was written, in part, to satisfy an already burgeoning public interest in the Brontë family. The Brontë story has been told and re-told many times since, with all manner of different emphases and interpretive slants. Right up to the present day it has been the ground for much dispute, not only within biography but also literary criticism, fiction, poetry, theatre and film.

With such great interest in the Brontës from such an early date, it was perhaps inevitable that Haworth would become a destination for literary pilgrimage and that the physical remains of the Brontës' lives would become revered and sought after as relics. The Brontës' father, Patrick, having outlived his wife and all six of his children, lived long enough to witness this, being generous enough to receive curious visitors when the mood took him, and cutting some of Charlotte's letters into snippets to satisfy requests for samples of her handwriting.

The Brontë Society was also established early, in 1893, committed to the '...preservation of artefacts of whatever nature of the Brontë family'; and so began the development of what is now the world's largest collection of Brontë-related manuscripts, letters, artworks, furniture, domestic artefacts and personal treasures. The first 'Museum of Brontë Relics' had been opened in 1889 by Francis and Robinson

Brown, cousins of Martha Brown, the Brontës' servant, above their Refreshment Rooms at 123 Main Street, Haworth. The Brontë Society opened its first museum above the Yorkshire Penny Bank, now the Tourist Information Centre, at the top of Main Street in 1895. Haworth Parsonage, the Brontës' home, opened as a museum in 1928 and has now welcomed more than seven million visitors: writers, artists, scholars, readers, and those simply moved by the story of the Brontës' lives.

Amongst some of the better known early visitors to Haworth was the novelist Virginia Woolf. Woolf came to Haworth in 1904 and wrote an account of her visit in the *Guardian* newspaper. She describes Haworth rather unflatteringly as 'dingy and commonplace' and refers to the Brontë Society's collection, then housed at the Yorkshire Penny Bank, as 'a pallid and inanimate collection of objects', commenting that 'An effort ought to be made to keep things out of these mausoleums'.

However, Woolf goes on, '...the choice often lies between them and destruction, so that we must be grateful for the care which has preserved much that is, under any circumstances, of deep interest'. She is profoundly moved by the 'personal relics'; dresses and shoes particularly:

The natural fate of such things is to die before the body that wore them, and because these, trifling and transient though they are, have survived, Charlotte Brontë the woman comes to life, and one forgets the chiefly memorable fact that she was a great writer.

Many more relics have been returned to Haworth and to the Parsonage Museum since Woolf made her pilgrimage, and the story of how the Brontë Society's collection has grown and developed is a fascinating one in its own right; complete with a colourful cast of characters (both heroes and villains), twists and turns that would seem melodramatic in fiction, and even an unresolved mystery or two. That collection is of course a great scholarly resource which has given us important new insights into the Brontës' lives and works. But as well as allowing us to access the Brontës as great writers, the collection also bears witness, in a powerfully moving way, to the Brontës as ordinary human beings. It is for this reason, just as much as the Brontës' literary achievements, that people continue to make the pilgrimage to Haworth; why these relics have such a powerful effect upon us, and why their history is so compelling.

Andrew McCarthy, Director, Brontë Parsonage Museum

In 1895 the Brontë Society opened its first museum on the upper floor of the Yorkshire Penny Bank, now the Tourist Information Centre, at the top of Haworth's Main Street. The Museum remained here until the Society acquired Haworth Parsonage in 1928.

Little by little, through the researches of this person or that, we have learned more and more of the Brontës, and on the other hand, their one time belongings are becoming more and more scattered... Unless a systematic effort be soon made to gather them together, I fear the carrying out of a scheme for a museum will become impossible...a necessary preliminary to all this is the establishment of a Brontë Society.

W. W. Yates, *The Dewsbury Reporter*, 1893

Brontë Relics: A Collection History

The publication of Mrs Gaskell's *The Life of Charlotte Brontë* in 1857, two years after Charlotte's death, generated a huge amount of interest in the lives of the Brontë family. Patrick Brontë, who lived long enough to see photographs of himself for sale in the Main Street alongside copies of his daughters' novels, would often cut Charlotte's letters into snippets to meet the many requests he received for samples of her handwriting. Charles Hale was one of the many Americans inspired to visit Haworth after reading Mrs Gaskell's biography. He arrived in the village shortly after Mr Brontë's death in 1861 when the Parsonage was being fitted out in preparation for the arrival of his successor, and reported that:

> *...Mr Nicholls in going away took nearly everything of especial value or interest which had belonged to his wife; but the remaining household effects were disposed of by public auction about three weeks ago. The sale was considered a matter of no consequence; it was not widely advertised nor largely attended.*

Hale was determined to acquire souvenirs of his visit, and proudly carried away the wire and crank of Mr Brontë's bell-pull and the lower sash of Charlotte Brontë's bedroom window.

A photograph of Patrick Brontë in old age, c.1860.

The largest collection of Brontë material in Haworth itself belonged to the family's servant, Martha Brown, who was on a visit to Nicholls's home in Ireland at the

Above: an early photograph of Haworth Parsonage, c.1860.

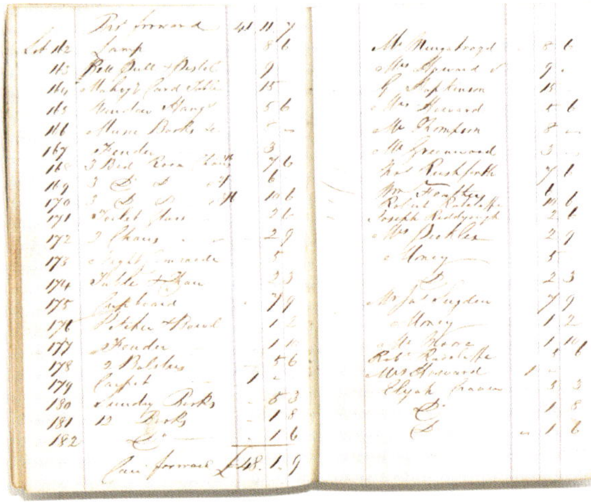

Right: catalogue for the sale at Haworth Parsonage, held on 1 and 2 October 1861.

time of Hale's visit. Martha was reluctant to part with her mementos, but following her death in 1880 the collection passed to her five sisters, and collectors began to arrive in the village. Amongst the most persistent of these was the Lancashire leather manufacturer William Law. Martha's relatives were sought out and often persuaded to part with their Brontë items. In 1886, following the death of Martha's brother-in-law Benjamin Binns, a sale was held at Saltaire which included 44 lots of original Brontë items which had passed to Binns' wife Ann. The sale sparked a growing sense amongst Brontë enthusiasts of the need to gather together and preserve the surviving possessions of the Brontës before the opportunity was lost for ever. The Brontë Society was formed in 1893 by a small group dedicated to promoting the Brontës' works and preserving what remained of the family's belongings.

A large collection of manuscripts and original Brontë items was released by the death of Arthur Bell Nicholls in 1906. Many of the items owned by Nicholls had already passed into the hands of the unscrupulous Thomas J. Wise, but some relics with which he had not been prepared to part during his lifetime were sold at Sotheby's in 1907. The Brontë Society was able to purchase a number of items at the sale.

The Brontë Society had opened their first museum in Haworth in 1895, but they hoped that one day they would be able to acquire the Parsonage, which in the years since Patrick Brontë's death had served as home to four of his successors. By 1927 the Society's collection had outgrown the small museum in Main Street, and at this time it was announced that the Church authorities were prepared to sell Haworth Parsonage for a sum of £3,000. The Parsonage was purchased by Sir James Roberts, a local boy-made-good, who had made a fortune in the textile industry. He also contributed a further sum towards the cost of fitting up the house as a museum and library. On 4 August 1928 thousands of people thronged Church Street to witness the official opening of the Brontë Parsonage Museum.

The acquisition of the Parsonage prompted many owners of Brontëana to return items to their original home. Other Brontë treasures entered the Parsonage collection by more circuitous means, and this catalogue looks at the fascinating story of how the Museum's collection came together.

Above: the crowded interior of the Main Street Museum.

Right: Sir James Roberts purchased Haworth Parsonage in 1928 and on 4 August, thousands turned out for the official opening of the Brontë Parsonage Museum.

Charlotte's rosewood and mother-of-pearl workbox, which includes compartments filled with fragments of textiles, buttons, silk ribbon, thread and needles.

A curious packet…containing an immense amount of manuscript in an inconceivably small space

Mrs Gaskell's *The Life of Charlotte Brontë*, 1857

A photograph of Charlotte Brontë's husband, Arthur Bell Nicholls.

Arthur Bell Nicholls

After the death of his beloved wife Charlotte, Arthur Bell Nicholls stayed at the Parsonage to care for Mr Brontë, his frail father-in-law, in the remaining years of his life. On the death of Mr Brontë in 1861 Arthur decided to return to his native Ireland. Having inherited all the Brontës' possessions, he took a number of Charlotte's manuscripts, personal mementos, drawings and letters with him. Other items were given to Martha Brown and her sister Tabitha before he left, and the household contents were sold in a local auction, which villagers attended with an eye for a useful and practical bargain rather than a Brontë relic.

Arthur became a farmer, married his cousin Mary Bell, and they lived at Hill House in Banagher, where Arthur paid tribute to his famous late wife by laying out Brontë first editions in glass cases, hanging drawings by all the sisters on the walls, and proudly displaying the famous Richmond portrait of Charlotte in the drawing-room. Branwell's now famous 'Pillar Portrait' of his three sisters was folded twice and placed on top of an old cupboard, where it was hidden until after Arthur's death. With it was a mysterious portrait of Emily Brontë, torn from another group portrait depicting Branwell and his sisters. The rest had been discarded, possibly owing to Arthur's lack of appreciation for Branwell's work. Arthur is believed to have seen a fair likeness in the Emily fragment, deciding him to keep it. This fragment, together with the 'Pillar Portrait', is now permanently displayed in London's National Portrait Gallery.

Mary Bell, Arthur's cousin and second wife.

Emily's pencil drawing of her dog Grasper, drawn from life when she was fifteen years old.

Christening mug which belonged to Emily.

Despite attempting to live a reclusive life on his Irish farm, Mr Nicholls and his Brontë collection became increasingly sought after by souvenir hunters, in particular the Brontë scholar and biographer Clement Shorter. Having acquired a number of Charlotte Brontë letters, Shorter sought to expand his collection of Brontë material, intending to publish a book of Charlotte's letters. In order to do this he would need the permission of the copyright holder, who was now Arthur.

Shorter travelled to Ireland in 1895 to meet Arthur and discuss with him his collection of Brontëana, both for purchase and publication. Acting partly on his 'friend' Thomas Wise's instructions, and with his financial backing, Shorter acquired important letters, manuscripts, and a small bundle of famous handmade 'little books', which Arthur had intended to burn. He also granted Shorter the 'exclusive right to publish any MSS I send you.'

Shorter's brief visit was seemingly a great success for all: he now held the copyright of the letters, Arthur and his wife were comfortably better off, and Wise possessed the actual manuscripts.

Both Arthur and Charlotte's lifelong friend Ellen Nussey believed that the manuscripts they sold to Wise would end up in a national collection which, Wise reassured them, would enhance 'the honor and reputation of their gloriously gifted writer,' and 'keep them safe for future generations'.

Nicholls had not passed his entire collection to Shorter and Wise, however: many items held memories of his late wife too dear for him to part with them, and he kept them.

On July 26, 1907, after Arthur's death, Sotheby's sold 58 lots of Brontëana on behalf of his widow. Mrs Nicholls gave away various items before she died, but many books, manuscripts, letters and drawings remained. With growing interest in both Britain and America for Brontëana, the auction raised £718, with high prices paid for signed and inscribed books. Lot 35, Charlotte's paintbox, was bought by the Brontë Society for £4 4s, and Lot 32, Emily's writing desk, was acquired by Henry Bonnell, an American collector who later bequeathed this along with his entire collection to the Parsonage Museum. Mrs Nicholls held a second sale of Brontëana at Sotheby's on June 19, 1914, including furniture from the Parsonage, Brontë books, notebooks used in Brussels, manuscripts, diary papers and tiny books filled with early writings. After her death the final Sotheby's auction on December 15, 1916, saw the last items of Arthur's beloved collection sold. Many of these have now returned to the collection at Haworth.

Left: white plaster medallion of Branwell Brontë in profile sculpted by his friend and biographer Joseph Bentley Leyland.

Below left: Charlotte Brontë's paintbox, probably dating from her school-days at Roe Head when she began to study art.

Below: Biblical sampler by Anne Brontë dated 23 January 1830.

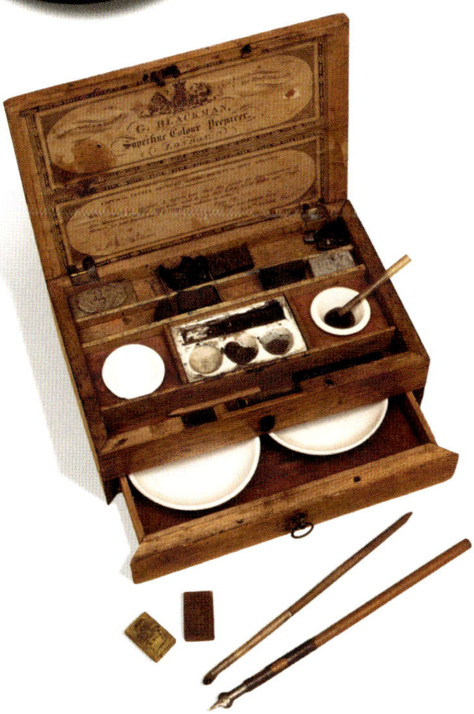

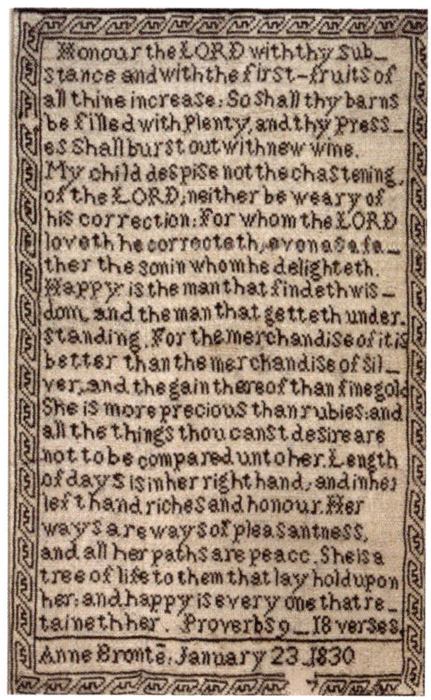

when I say so – it seems to me that y[ou]
will hardly hear me – all the ~~heaving~~ r[oaring]
of the Channel, heaving & roaring between
must deaden the sound –

go-o-d-b-y-e

C B

...if you adopt the course we wish you to do, you will be doing the thing most calculated to serve the interests of your dead friend, & will preserve these letters for all time, intact, as a lasting memorial of the friendship she bore you.

Thomas J. Wise letter to Ellen Nussey, 14 November, 1892

A photograph of Ellen Nussey.

Ellen Nussey

MOST OF THE surviving Brontë letters are written by Charlotte, and many of these are to her close friend Ellen Nussey (1817-1897). Charlotte and Ellen met in 1831 when they were both pupils at Roe Head School, near Dewsbury, and corresponded for the rest of Charlotte's life. When Charlotte married Arthur Bell Nicholls he was shocked at the confidential nature of their correspondence.

'Arthur says such letters as mine ought never to be kept, they are dangerous as Lucifer matches...' Charlotte had written shortly after her marriage, and he had insisted that she extract a promise from Ellen to destroy all future correspondence. Despite her promise, Ellen failed to comply with Nicholls's request, and after Charlotte's death claimed to have kept over five hundred of her letters. It is on these surviving letters that much of our knowledge of the Brontës' everyday lives is based.

Unlike Nicholls, who had opted to live in relative obscurity in his native Ireland, Ellen remained in the Birstall area, where she was sought out by Brontë enthusiasts, collectors and biographers, all eager to gain access to her hoard. Many of the letters had already been loaned to Mrs Gaskell, and quoted extensively in *The Life of Charlotte Brontë* (1857). Ellen was unhappy with Gaskell's biography and hoped for a new account of Charlotte's life which would minimise the 'fearful history of her brother'.

In 1887 the letters were loaned to J. Horsfall Turner, a local antiquarian and author, for a proposed edition of Charlotte's letters which it was intended would appear after Ellen's death. She was shocked when she learnt that printed sheets of the new

Opposite page: in this illustrated letter to Ellen sent from Brussels, Charlotte caricatured herself as an ugly dwarf-like figure.

This miniature portrait is said to be of Ellen Nussey by Charlotte. It was formerly owned by Ellen and included in the sale of her effects.

The catalogue for the sale held at Ellen's home, Moor Lane House, in 1898.

edition had already been produced and many personal references retained, as well as by discovering that copyright rested with Nicholls. Since his distaste for making public his wife's personal letters was well known, and since Ellen had defied Nicholls by keeping them against his wishes, it seemed unlikely he would sanction publication. After a great deal of hostility the edition was suppressed. Ellen regained her original letters (although she claimed Turner did not return them all), plus the thousands of printed sheets, which she destroyed. Very few copies survived the bonfire.

By the time Ellen met the journalist Clement Shorter in 1892 she was 75 years old, and dissatisfied with the biographical accounts of her friend which had appeared over the years. Anxious both to set the record straight and to ensure the preservation of her letters, Shorter suggested she sell them to his friend Thomas J. Wise, a respected bibliographer and book collector, who was also willing to make them available for Shorter to produce a new study of Charlotte's life. Wise possessed a fine collection of nineteenth-century manuscripts, and had already arranged to purchase Charlotte's letters to W. S. Williams. In a letter dated 14 November, 1892, he wrote to assure Ellen of his plans:

I do not intend that these shall ever be scattered, but have made arrangements to bequeath them to the Nation & at my death I propose them to go to South Kensington Museum, there to occupy a room close to the Foster library. You will thus see that if you adopt the course we wish you to do, you will be doing the thing most calculated to serve the interests of your dead friend, & will preserve these letters for all time, intact, as a lasting memorial of the friendship she bore you.

For Ellen, living in genteel poverty, it must have seemed an ideal solution, and she gratefully accepted Wise's proposal, along with a cheque for £125. Within a year of the letters leaving her hands, however, she was shocked to discover them appearing in the saleroom. It is an indication of how much she trusted Wise that she did not suspect him, initially blaming Horsfall Turner instead. Moreover, the bullying tactics Wise employed in his later dealings with Ellen discouraged her attempts to hold him to account for his breach of promise.

Ellen Nussey died on 26 November, 1897, at the age of 80. Her connection with the Brontës lent an added interest to the sale of her effects at her former home, Moor Lane House in Gomersal. Those attending must have been disappointed to find so few Brontë items included in the sale, for most had already passed through the hands of Thomas J. Wise.

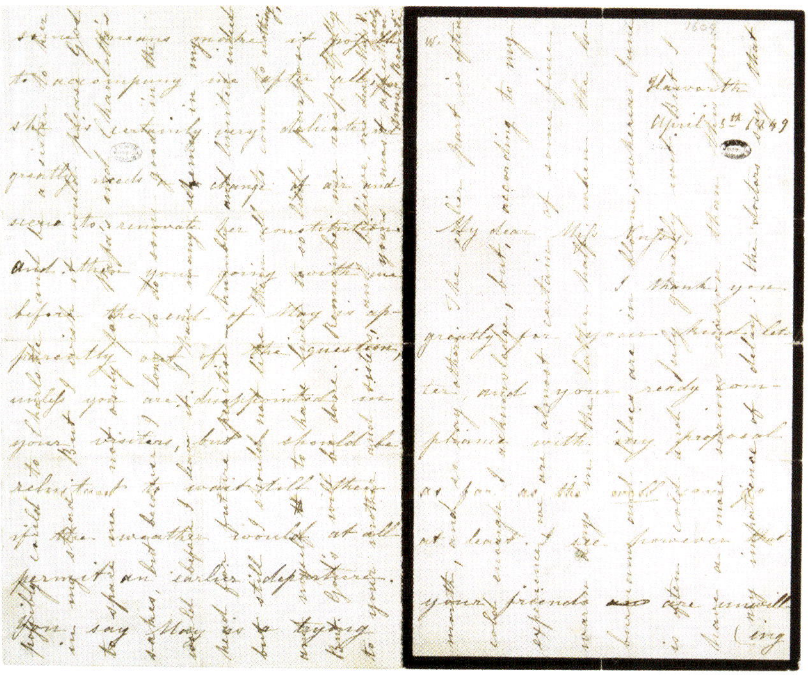
means making it possible
to accompany me after all, for
she is certainly very delicate and
greatly needs a change of air and
scene to renovate her constitution.
And then your going with me
before the end of May is apparently out of the question,
unless you are disappointed in
your visitors, but I should be
reluctant to wait till then
if the weather would at all
permit an earlier departure.
You say May is a trying

Haworth
April 5th 1849
My dear Miss Nussey,
I thank you
greatly for your kind letter, and your ready compliance with my proposal
as far as the will can go
at least. I see however that
your friends are unwill-
(ing

Above: Anne Brontë's last letter, dated 5 April, 1849, in which she requests Ellen's company on a visit to Scarborough where it was hoped the sea air would restore her health.

Right: a smelling salts bottle which belonged to Mrs Brontë. The bottle was donated to the Brontë Society by Emma Cortazzo, a friend of Ellen's, who claimed that the bottle had also 'been loved and used' by Anne Brontë in her last days.

Anne Bronte
By my daughter Charlotte
P. Brontë Minr.

Martha had had several visitors who were anxious to see her treasures, some of whom made tempting offers to induce her to part with them. These, however, she firmly declined, as she wished to keep them in her own possession as long as she lived…

William Scruton, *Thornton and the Brontës*, 1898

Photograph of Martha Brown taken towards the end of her life.

MARTHA BROWN AND THE BRONTËS

MARTHA BROWN WAS one of the six daughters of John Brown, sexton of Haworth Church, who came to the Parsonage at the age of eleven to assist the elderly servant, Tabitha Aykroyd. 'From my first entering the house,' she later claimed, 'I was always recognised and treated as a member of the family.' Martha remained with the Brontës for many years, eventually becoming housekeeper, and leaving only after Patrick Brontë's death in 1861. Patrick left Martha the sum of thirty pounds – three times her annual salary – as a 'token of regard for long and faithful services to me and my children.' She also inherited a collection of letters, drawings, inscribed copies of the Brontës' works, and many personal belongings, testament to the friendship between herself and the Brontë family. She remained on friendly terms with Charlotte's husband, Arthur Bell Nicholls, corresponding with him, and visiting him at his home in Ireland. When not staying with Nicholls and his second wife, Martha spent long periods living with her married sisters, before renting a cottage of her own at Haworth.

Martha's name was familiar to readers of *The Life of Charlotte Brontë*. She was extremely proud of her association with the Brontës, and happy to talk about the family and show her treasured collection to the many enthusiasts who beat a path to her door. One of these was William Scruton, the Bradford antiquarian and author, who interviewed Martha in June 1879. He wrote how Martha *had treasured up many valuable and interesting mementos of the Brontë family, several of which had been given to her by Mr Brontë…Among the more interesting of them was an old portfolio*

Opposite page: a pencil drawing of Anne Brontë by Charlotte, dated 17 April 1833. The drawing was owned by Martha Brown, eventually passing to her sister Tabitha.

Above: this veil of white embroidered net was attached to the rim of the bonnet worn by Charlotte on her wedding day. The veil was kept by Martha Brown and eventually purchased from her great-great niece Betty Scarborough.

Right: this silk dress is made up of a separate skirt and jacket, and was worn by Charlotte when she set out on her honeymoon tour in 1854. The dress was purchased from Ellen Binns in 1907.

filled with the pencil drawings and water-colour sketches of Patrick Branwell and his sisters. But still more valuable than these, to our mind, were the miniature magazines in Charlotte's handwriting, written in such small characters as to be scarcely decipherable without the aid of a glass.

The last glimpse we have of Martha is provided by Sydney Biddell, an admirer of the Brontës, who visited her at Haworth on 5 September, 1879. Biddell made notes about his visit in the margins of his copy of *The Life of Charlotte Brontë*. Beneath Martha's signature he noted: 'I called and was with Martha Brown for three-and-a-half hours...' During that time Martha showed Biddell her mementos of the Brontë family, and he made further notes, recording details of some items. Biddell's copy of the biography is now held at the Brontë Parsonage Museum, and provides a useful record of some of the items at one time owned by Martha.

Within six months of Biddell's visit Martha had died and was buried in the churchyard at Haworth, close to the south wall of the Parsonage garden. Although she had sold selected Brontë items over the years, presumably on occasions of financial necessity, her collection remained almost intact. In accordance with the terms of her will her Brontëana was divided equally amongst her five sisters, and in this way gradually dispersed.

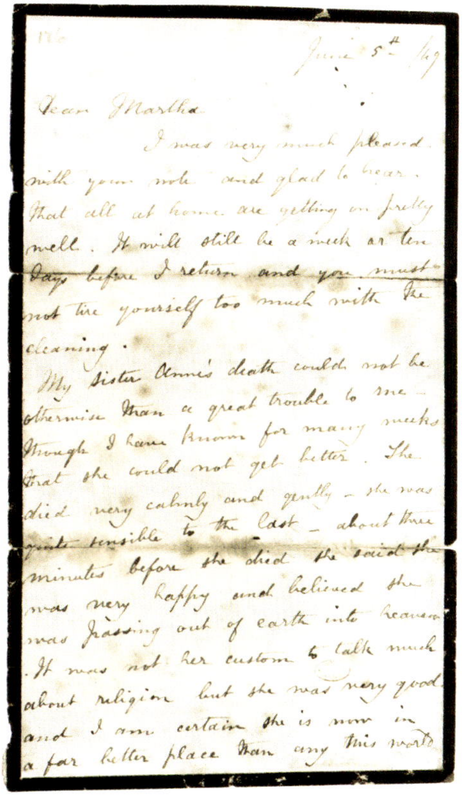
June 5th 49

Dear Martha

I was very much pleased with your note and glad to hear that all at home are getting on pretty well. It will still be a week or ten days before I return and you must not tire yourself too much with the cleaning.

My sister Anne's death could not be otherwise than a great trouble to me though I have known for many weeks that she could not get better. She died very calmly and gently – she was quite sensible to the last – about three minutes before she died she said she was very happy and believed she was passing out of earth into heaven. It was not her custom to talk much about religion but she was very good and I am certain she is now in a far better place than any this world

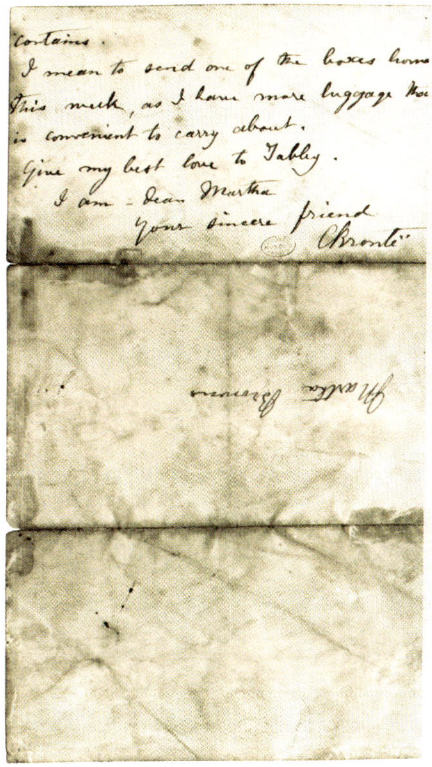
contains.

I mean to send one of the boxes home this week, as I have more luggage than is convenient to carry about.

Give my best love to Tabby.

I am – Dear Martha

Your sincere friend

C Brontë

Martha Brown

William Scruton, who was shown Martha Brown's collection of Brontëana, wrote: *Some of the relics were linked with associations that rendered them priceless. One of these was a letter which she had received from Miss Brontë soon after the death of her sister Anne.* This letter, dated 5 June 1849, is now in the collection of the Brontë Parsonage Museum.

Tabitha Ratcliffe photographed with some of her Brontë relics.

Some, we are somewhat astonished to learn, money will buy, if the price is satisfactory.

Whitely Turner, *A Spring-Time Saunter*, 1905

Photograph of Francis Brown, cousin of the Brontës' servant, Martha Brown.

THE BROWN AND BINNS FAMILIES

BRADFORD WRITER WILLIAM Scruton noted in 1879 that the Brontës' servant Martha Brown 'had had many opportunities of parting with her treasures', but that she kept most through sentimental attachment. Upon her death, however, the collection was divided between her five sisters, Ann, Eliza, Tabitha, Mary and Hannah. Gradually the treasures began to disperse.

Tourists to the area, hot on the Brontë trail, often tracked down the five sisters from the 1880s onwards; many were allowed to view the relics. A visitor in 1882 records Mrs Ratcliffe (Martha's sister Tabitha) *showing of her "bits of things" with loving fervour, spreading them on the table to my view. A little wooden foot stool and an inkstained writing desk seemed, she said, to go together, for "Miss Emily always carried the stool into the garden or put it before the kitchen fire and then put the desk on her knee when she was about writing".*

The Halifax journalist Whitely Turner also visited Tabitha, and was shown Anne's workbox, the Parsonage kitchen candlesticks, Mr Brontë's willow-pattern mug, and an oval-shaped brooch of Anne's, containing Charlotte's hair. But by now the treasures were not always just for show. 'Some, we are somewhat astonished to learn, money will buy, if the price is satisfactory,' recorded Mr Turner.

Their essential poverty meant that the Brown sisters – however loyal to the Brontës' memory – were vulnerable to cash offers; many artefacts were sold to souvenir hunters.

The eldest sister, Ann, was married, stormily, to Benjamin Binns, a tailor. Benjamin had been a friend of Branwell's, regularly fetching for him a periodical called *Bell's Sporting Life* from the Shake Hands Beer House in Keighley. Martha had lived with Ann and Benjamin at Saltaire for nine years, but departed to Haworth to live alone when she could no longer stand their quarrelling.

When Benjamin died in 1886 the Binns' Brontë relics were sold, presumably to help support his widow. Under the hammer were 40 lots, described as 'Books and Works of Art by the Brontë Family, and Property Originally in their Possession.' These included Emily's watercolour of Anne's dog Flossy; letters from Patrick and Charlotte to Martha; Patrick's spectacles; Charlotte's boots, shawl, and even her corset.

Alfred Gledhill, a 'general agent' based in nearby Keighley, was an early and keen collector, and managed to buy many items, some of which he later exhibited at a series of 'Keighley Conversaziones' held at the Keighley Mechanics' Institute in January 1889. He then sold his collection to Martha Brown's cousins Francis and Robinson Brown.

The Brown Brothers – sons of Martha's uncle William – were an enterprising pair who ran the Refreshment Rooms at 123 Main Street, Haworth. In 1889 they decided it would benefit trade to open a Museum of Brontë Relics above the shop. There they displayed not only items bought from Alfred Gledhill and from Martha's sisters, but also from Ellen Nussey and William Scruton.

'Visitors to Haworth should not fail to see the Collection of BRONTË RELICS, which is the largest that has ever been got together,' ran their advertisement. Sadly it failed to attract the crowds.

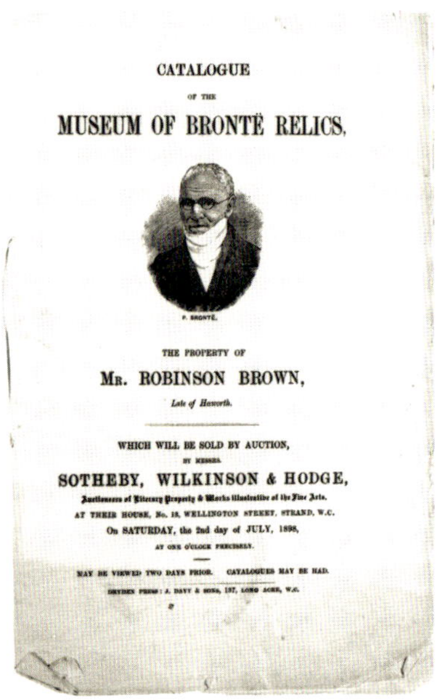

CATALOGUE

OF THE

MUSEUM OF BRONTË RELICS,

P. BRONTË.

THE PROPERTY OF

MR. ROBINSON BROWN,

Late of Haworth.

WHICH WILL BE SOLD BY AUCTION,

BY MESSRS.

SOTHEBY, WILKINSON & HODGE,

Auctioneers of Literary Property & Works illustrative of the Fine Arts,

AT THEIR HOUSE, No. 13, WELLINGTON STREET, STRAND, W.C.

On SATURDAY, the 2nd day of JULY, 1898,

AT ONE O'CLOCK PRECISELY.

MAY BE VIEWED TWO DAYS PRIOR. CATALOGUES MAY BE HAD.

DRYDEN PRESS: J. DAVY & SONS, 137, LONG ACRE, W.C.

Left: catalogue of the Brown collection of Brontë relics auctioned at Sotheby's, 1898.

Below: a multi-coloured patchwork quilt worked by the Brontë sisters, which was included in the sale at Sotheby's in 1898.

A portrait of John Brown by Branwell, c.1835-1839. This portrait is believed to have passed to Brown's daughter, Ann Binns, and was purchased from the Binns family in 1911.

Above: watercolour of a dog, said to be Flossy, attributed to Emily Brontë.

Right: this portrait of Charlotte Brontë by J. H. Thompson was purchased from Francis Brown's daughter in 1950, along with several other Brontë items.

With trade slow, the Browns packed up and moved the collection, first to Blackpool, where their bad luck continued, then to the Chicago Exhibition of 1893, hoping they might find rich Americans to pay good prices for their artefacts.

Their asking price of £500 was too high even for rich Americans, however, and certainly too high for the fledgling Brontë Society, whose representatives tried in vain to negotiate a lower figure so that items could be rescued for their own new museum.

In 1898 the brothers made a last-ditch attempt to sell their Brontë relics at Sotheby's in London, but the results were disappointing, and many lots failed to sell at all. The Brontë Society managed to buy Emily's watercolour of Flossy for just £12, and an unfinished quilt worked by all three sisters for just £1.2s. In all, members spent just £20 on a handful of lots – some for mere shillings – but these formed the Society's first major purchase, and the foundation of the Brontë collection you see today.

Items that failed to sell, including J. H. Thompson's oil portrait of Charlotte, passed to Francis Brown's daughter, from whom the Brontë Society eventually managed to purchase them in 1950.

Of the lots which went missing, many have resurfaced over the years, and been donated to or purchased by the Brontë Parsonage Museum. Almost certainly there are still more treasures in attics and basements, tucked away in drawers and chests, still waiting to be rediscovered.

Charlotte's writing desk and some of its original contents. It was purchased at Sotheby's sale of the Nicholls collection and later donated to the Brontë Museum by Alexander Murray Smith, George Smith's son.

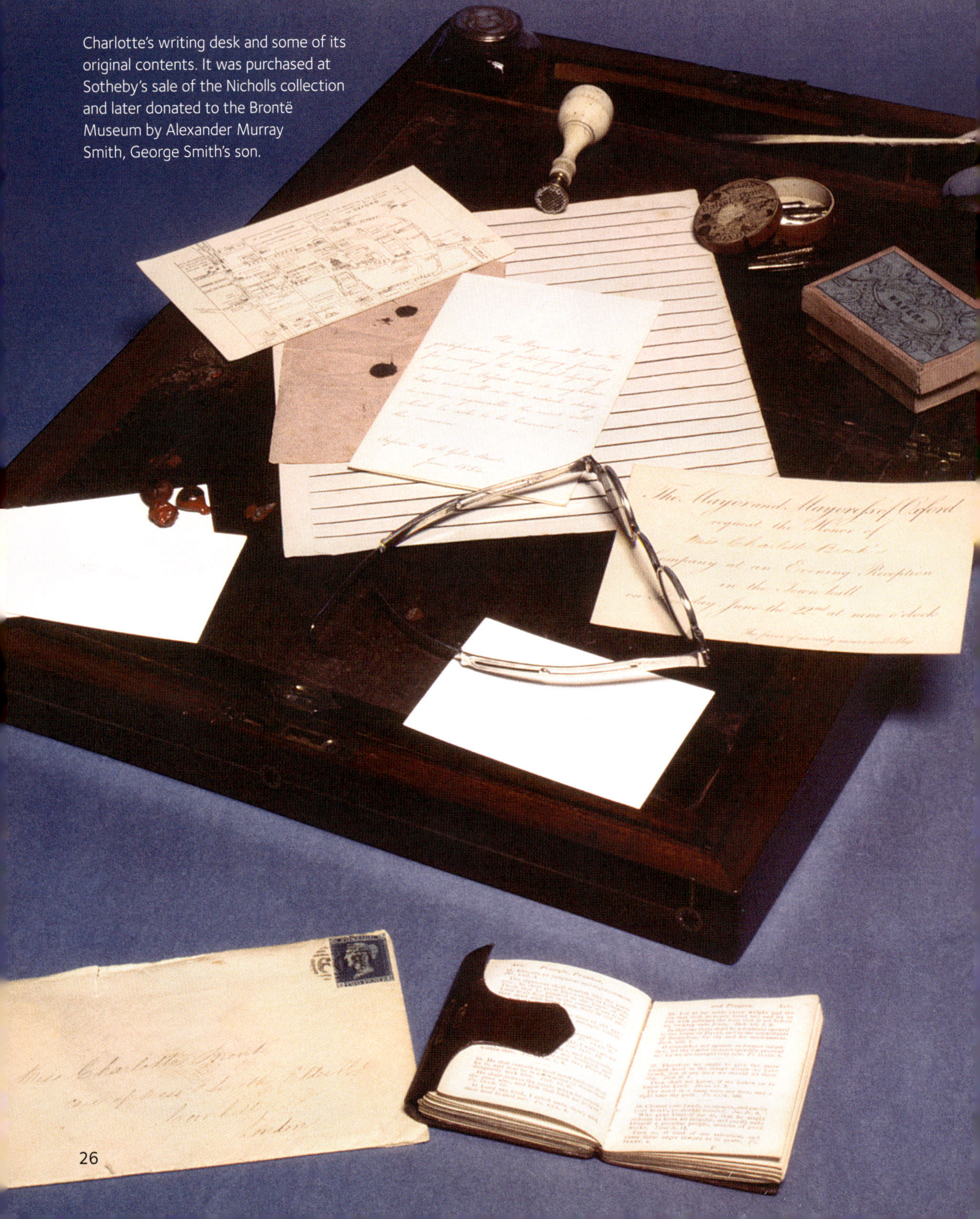

After breakfast on Sunday morning I took the manuscript of Jane Eyre *to the library and began to read it. The story quickly took me captive...*

George Smith, *A Memoir*, 1902

Portrait of George Smith, Charlotte's publisher.

GEORGE SMITH

THE ORIGINAL HANDWRITTEN manuscripts for Charlotte Brontë's novels only exist today because they were cannily saved by Charlotte's publisher George Smith.

In 1847 Charlotte posted off *Jane Eyre* to the dynamic 23-year-old publisher, who had not long since taken over his father's firm Smith, Elder & Co., and was seeking to make a name for himself.

He describes his first encounter with the novel, on a day he should have been lunching with a friend:

After breakfast on Sunday morning I took the manuscript of Jane Eyre *to the library and began to read it. The story quickly took me captive. At twelve o'clock my horse came to the door, but I could not put the book down. I scribbled two or three lines to my friend, saying I was very sorry circumstances had occurred to prevent my meeting him, sent the note off by my groom, and went on reading the manuscript. Presently the servant came to tell me that lunch was waiting; I asked him to bring me a sandwich and a glass of wine and still went on with* Jane Eyre. *Dinner came; for me the meal was a very hasty one, and before I went to bed that night I had finished the manuscript. My literary judgement was perfectly satisfied.*

The manuscript was soon followed by Charlotte herself, who, with Anne, travelled to London to convince George Smith that the Brontë novels were written by three separate people, after a rumour circulated that there was, in fact, only one author using three separate names.

Smith took an instant liking to the sisters, though he was charmed more by their personalities than their looks. He describes them as 'two rather quaintly dressed little ladies, pale-faced and anxious looking,' and noted of Charlotte: 'It may seem strange

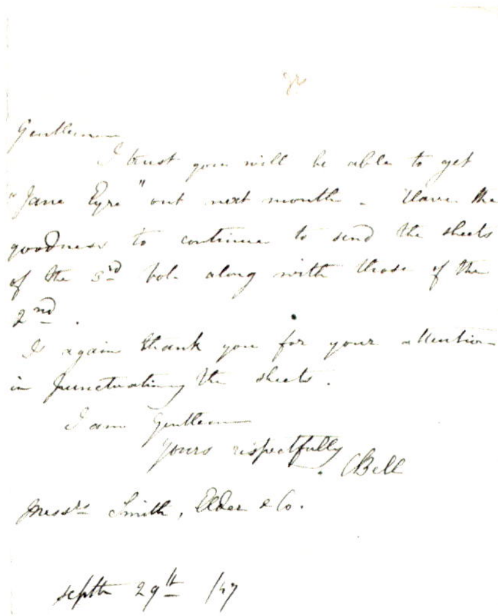
Gentlemen
I trust you will be able to get "Jane Eyre" out next month. Have the goodness to continue to send the sheets of the 3rd vol. along with those of the 2nd.
I again thank you for your attention in punctuating the sheets.
I am Gentlemen
Yours respectfully C Bell
Messrs Smith, Elder & Co.

Septbr 29th /47

Above: a plait of Anne Brontë's hair and an accompanying note by her father were placed in an envelope and found amongst the contents of Charlotte's desk. The note reads: 'Anne Brontë / May 22 1833 / Aged 13 years.'

Right: Charlotte Brontë letter to Smith, Elder & Co., 29 September, 1847.

that the possession of genius did not lift her above the weakness of an excessive anxiety about her personal appearance; but I believe that she would have given all her genius and her fame to have been beautiful.'

Smith was a generous, charming and energetic man, who treated his authors to lavish presents, star-studded dinners and trips to view the opera from his box at Covent Garden. He invited Charlotte to London to stay with his family on four occasions, and his mother and sisters took her to visit galleries and museums, and go shopping with them.

He was also unmarried, and, though he was eight years younger than Charlotte, she was clearly attracted to him, writing to her friend Ellen Nussey in January 1851:

Were there no vast barrier of age, fortune etc. there is perhaps enough personal regard to make things possible which are now impossible. If men and women married because they like each others' temper, look, conversation, nature and so on – and if besides, years were more closely equal – the chance you allude to might be admitted as a chance – but other reasons regulate matrimony – reasons of convenience, of connection, of money. Meantime I am content to have him as a friend – and pray to God to continue to me the commonsense to look on one so young, so rising and so hopeful in no other light...

Many years after Charlotte's death the author Mrs Humphry Ward asked Smith directly whether he had ever been in love with Charlotte. He replied:

No, I was never in the least bit in love with Charlotte Brontë...The truth is I never could have loved any woman who had not some charm or grace of person, and Charlotte Brontë had none. I liked her and was interested by her, and I admired her – especially when she was in Yorkshire and I was in London. I never was coxcomb enough to suppose that she was in love with me. But I believe that my mother was at one time rather alarmed.

Smith's mother had no cause for alarm, however. In February 1854 he married the pretty, very sociable, eminently suitable Elizabeth Blakeway. Four months later Charlotte herself was married to Arthur Bell Nicholls, her father's curate.

Smith's career went from strength to strength, as he published Thackeray, Mrs Gaskell and Harriet Martineau – all met through his connection with Charlotte Brontë – and began both the successful *Cornhill Magazine* and the evening newspaper the *Pall Mall Gazette*.

When he died in 1901 he left to his widow the manuscripts of three of Charlotte's novels: *Jane Eyre*, *Shirley* and *Villette*, as well as a large collection of letters, most from Charlotte, but also some from her father, and from Arthur Bell Nicholls. The manuscripts for Emily and Anne's novels – published by Thomas Cautley Newby, and partly funded by them, to the tune of £50 per novel – have never been found, and were, presumably, destroyed by their publisher.

George Smith's Brontëana collection eventually passed to his grand-daughter Elizabeth Seton Gordon, who in 1974 donated most of it to the Brontë Parsonage Museum. As well as the manuscripts and letters the collection included several drawings by Charlotte, passed on to George Smith's son by Arthur Bell Nicholls' second wife Mary.

With them was an astonishing find: a photograph, inscribed on the back: 'Within a year of CB's death', and dated 1854, the year of Charlotte's honeymoon. Whether it was a honeymoon picture, to match that of her husband taken at the same time, or whether it was intended by George Smith for an edition of one of Charlotte's novels, is unknown. It is the only photograph in existence that is almost certainly of Charlotte.

Left: this 'little book' by Charlotte is the September issue of *Blackwood's Young Men's Magazine*, written in August 1829. It was acquired by George Smith and bequeathed to the Museum by his grand-daughter.

Right: a carte-de-visite photograph believed to be of Charlotte Brontë. The photograph was part of a bequest from Elizabeth Seton Gordon, the grand-daughter of George Smith.

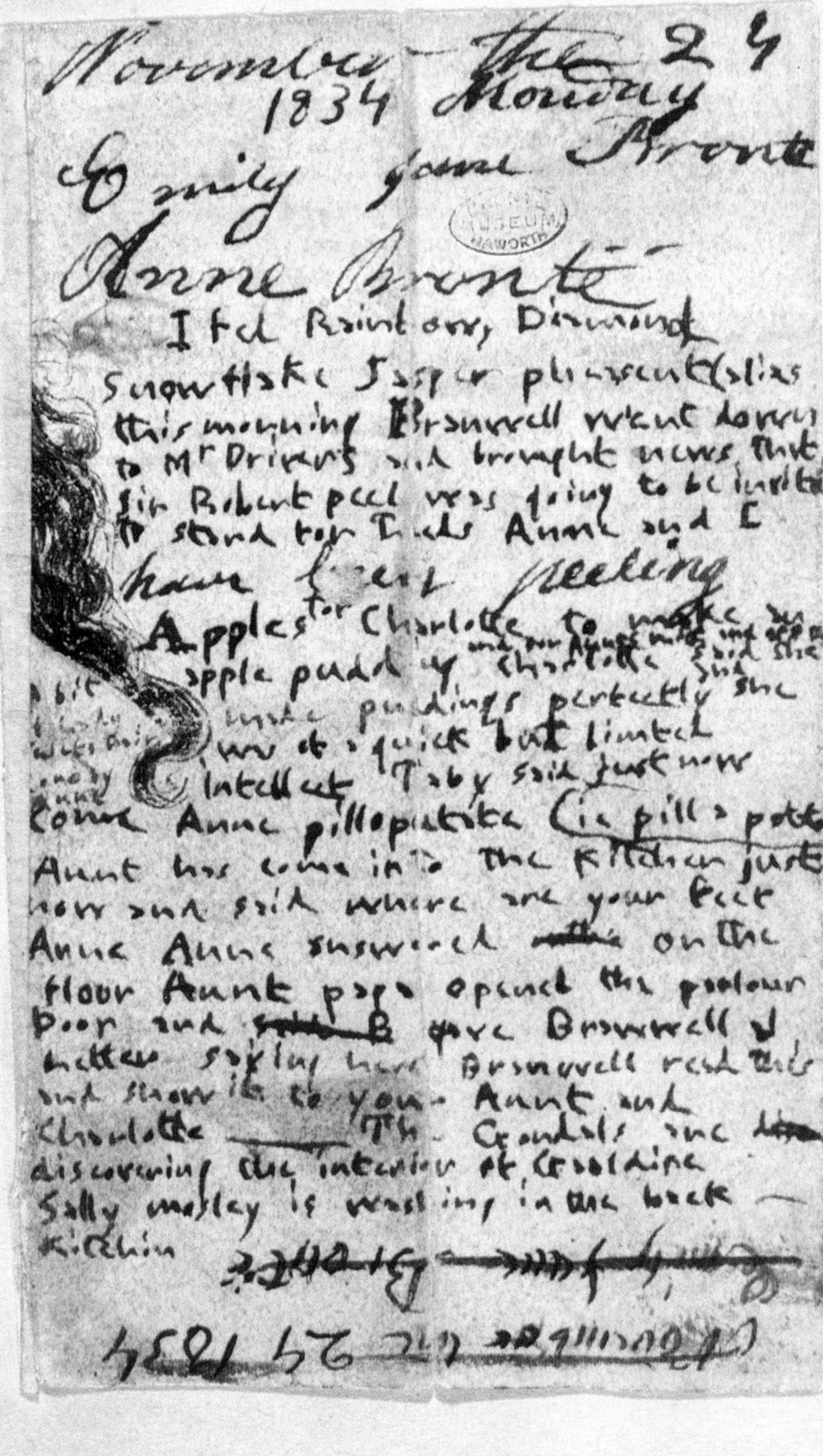
November the 24
1834 Monday
Emily Jane Brontë
Anne Brontë
I fed Rainbow, Diamond
Snowflake Jasper pheasent (alias
this morning Branwell went down
to Mr Driver's and brought news that
Sir Robert peel was going to be invited
to stand for Leeds Anne and I
have been peeling
Apples for Charlotte to make us
an apple pudding and for Aunt nuts and apples Charlotte said she
made puddings perfectly and she
was of a quick but limited
intellect Taby said just now
Come Anne pillopatate (ie pill a potate
Aunt has come into the Kitchen just
now and said where are your feet
Anne Anne answered On the
floor Aunt papa opened the parlour
Door and gave Branwell a
Letter saying here Branwell read this
and show it to your Aunt and
Charlotte — The Gondals are
discovering the interior of Gaaldine
Sally mosley is washing in the back
Kitchen
Emily Jane Brontë
November the 24 1834

It will be a splendid gift! But what a loss to America!

Journalist for the *Philadelphia Public Ledger*, 1906

A photograph of Henry Bonnell.

Henry Houston Bonnell

Some of the Brontë Parsonage Museum's greatest treasures once belonged to Henry Houston Bonnell of Philadelphia. Bonnell was a remarkable and generous man, whose life was devoted to literature and religion. He was an only child, born in 1859, and shortly after his birth his father left for California to pursue a career in gold-mining and land-agenting. By the time he returned home a few years later the family had enough money to last them the rest of their lives.

Henry attended one of the best schools in Philadelphia, then began studying literature at Pennsylvania University in 1880, later achieving a Master's degree there. A young millionaire with no need to work, Henry led a comfortable life, and grew into an educated, religious and well-read man, with a passion for book-collecting. A career with publishing firm Dodd, Mead & Co. in New York seemed the perfect occupation.

For forty years Dodd, Mead & Co. published religious works, but during Bonnell's time there they expanded their catalogue, branching out to publish authors such as Joseph Conrad, H. G. Wells and G. K. Chesterton. Bonnell even published his own first work with them in 1885, a booklet titled *Cremation: Scientifically and Religiously Considered.* He later went on to publish a critical work on Charlotte Brontë, Jane Austen and George Eliot.

Opposite page: this is the first in a series of diary papers written jointly by Emily and Anne Brontë. The sketch includes a rough drawing of a lock of hair by Anne Brontë.

Right: the earliest known example of Charlotte's prose writing with accompanying watercolour illustrations. The short story was written for her sister Anne, and is the first of a number of miniature books the Brontës made as children.

It was during Bonnell's time in New York City that he began his extensive book collection. Frequent visits to auctions and book dealers ignited his passion to amass rare and interesting books for the library at his home in the exclusive Chestnut Hill area of Philadelphia, and from 1890, when he was able to retire, he spent the rest of his life collecting and writing. His reputation as a monied private collector became known to dealers on both sides of the Atlantic, and before long they were offering him first editions and rarities. But although his collection was diverse, including volumes of travel, poetry and prose fiction by authors from the seventeenth to the nineteenth century, he did not widely collect manuscripts. In fact, Bonnell did not own one item of memorabilia or manuscript relating to any author apart from the Brontës.

Bonnell's first opportunity to purchase Brontë manuscripts arose in 1895 when some early manuscripts, letters and juvenilia – formerly part of Arthur Bell Nicholls' collection – came up for sale. Other early Brontë purchases are likely to have been through Thomas J. Wise, although Bonnell would not have known their unfortunate history.

Bonnell's first gift to the Brontë Society was in 1907: a pair of silver-rimmed spectacles in a shagreen case, once belonging to Mr Brontë. This was just one of forty lots he bought at the Sotheby's sale of Arthur Bell Nicholls' Brontë artefacts the same year. But it wasn't until 1916 that Bonnell first publicly announced he was to donate his collection to The Brontë Society after his death. An article in the *Philadelphia Public Ledger* exclaimed, 'It will be a splendid gift! But what a loss to America!'

As far as Bonnell was concerned, Haworth Parsonage was a literary shrine. He could have donated the world's largest collection of Brontëana to one of many institutions

Emily Brontë's portable writing desk with original contents including sealing wafers, blobs of sealing wax, wooden pen shafts, steel nibs, envelopes, acrostics, a concert programme, Belgian coins and five reviews of *Wuthering Heights*.

Watercolour drawing by Charlotte Brontë of a young woman holding a rose, titled *Portrait of a French Brunette*, dated 14 May 1833.

Above: one of Branwell's ink sketches of an imaginary character called Zamorna, drawn in 1835.

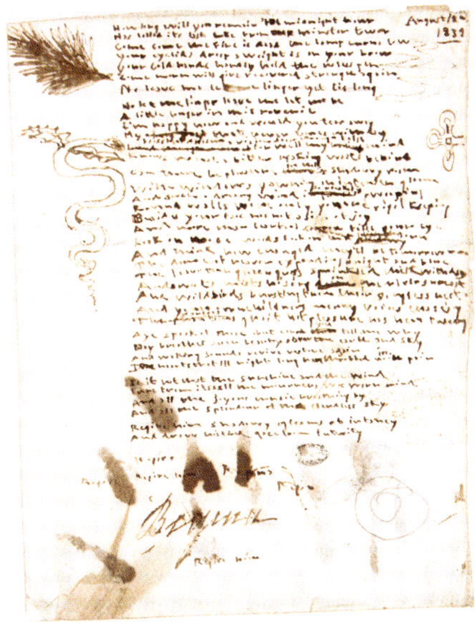

Right: this poem by Emily Brontë is one of a collection bound together in a volume of her work.

around the world, but he chose Haworth. He had faith that those who shared his passion would make the pilgrimage to see the home of the Brontë family and fully appreciate his carefully chosen relics, and hoped he would encourage others to donate as well, which he certainly did.

Henry was a bachelor for most of his life, but married in 1900 at the age of forty-one. His wife Ethel died three years later, leaving Bonnell to bring up their daughter Mariana, then in 1915, aged fifty-six, he married again, this time to a woman half his age, Helen Safford, who also grew up in a privileged family.

Bonnell died suddenly from a heart attack in 1926. Under the terms of his will his widow Helen despatched 336 items to The Brontë Parsonage Museum, retaining eighty herself. Each one is an absolute treasure. They include fifteen Emily Brontë poems, her writing desk filled with paraphernalia, first editions of each published novel, numerous 'little books', French essays, thirty-four drawings and watercolours, fifty Charlotte Brontë manuscripts, juvenile poems and short stories, nine poems by Anne Brontë and twenty by Branwell, over one hundred key Charlotte Brontë letters, and books from the Parsonage shelves, including Bibles, Emily's prayer book, Anne's book of Christian poets and Branwell's music book. Mrs Bonnell later donated the remaining items to the Pierpont Morgan Library in New York.

The Brontë Society can now claim to have the largest collection of Brontëana in the world, something which is largely due to Henry Houston Bonnell. Without his generosity we would know a great deal less about the Brontë family today.

Charlotte Brontë's writing desk, formerly part of the Law collection, was sold at Sotheby's in 2009. The successful bidder later donated it to the Museum, along with a pair of sugar tongs and a pen holder.

He preferred to live in the company of his books and pictures, and he had a fine collection of both.

Rochdale Observer, 3 August 1901

a great interest in the Y.M.C.A. He wa

Sir Alfred Joseph Law

also prominent in Lancashire Freemasonr

Sir Alfred J. Law, from his obituary in *The Yorkshire Post*.

THE LAW COLLECTION

WILLIAM LAW WAS a Lancashire flannel manufacturer whose financial success enabled him to build one of the world's most important and fascinating collections of Brontëana.

He led a very private life at his home, 'Honresfeld', near Littleborough in Rochdale, where his rare editions and Brontë manuscripts were housed in a library along with a Shakespeare Quarto and First Folio, manuscripts by Sir Walter Scott, and a spectacular display of paintings by Turner, Rembrandt and Hunt.

Law's Brontë archive was impressive, including drawings, 'little books', poetry manuscripts, letters and personal possessions of Charlotte, Emily, Anne and Branwell. He took frequent trips to Haworth in search of more Brontë relics for his collection, and managed to purchase a number of items from locals who knew the Brontë family well, such as joiner William Wood, and Tabitha Ratcliffe, sister of their servant Martha Brown. He contacted Arthur Bell Nicholls in the hope of acquiring a copy of *Wuthering Heights* with annotations by Emily Brontë herself, for which he was prepared to pay £50, an impressive sum of money in 1895. It is still not known whether this copy exists.

When the first Brontë museum opened in 1895, William Law donated an oil painting, *Jacob's Dream*, by Branwell, which he acquired from William Wood, who had made some items of furniture for the Brontës at the Parsonage, and repaired others. Other objects Law loaned for exhibitions, including Emily Brontë's own copy of *Poems*, from 1846, complete with her annotations.

When he died in 1901 Law's house and entire collection were inherited by his brother and business partner Alfred, then after Alfred's death in 1913, by his nephew, also called Alfred.

Sir Alfred Joseph Law was born in 1860, the son of John Law, William's brother.

He continued to run the family business, holding the position of Governing Director for a number of years, and was well liked by his employees. He served as MP for Rochdale from 1918 to 1922, and was knighted for his contribution to political life.

The librarian Davidson Cook was the first to inspect Alfred Law's magnificent hoard at Honresfeld in 1925. It's difficult to imagine the excitement he must have felt at being the first to record the many hidden treasures: Charlotte Brontë's writing desk 'crammed with relics' including 'several of the famous little MS books,' and an extremely rare leather-bound poetry notebook inscribed 'E.J.B', dated February 1844. Law had a particular fondness for Emily's work, and these were just a few of the jewels Cook found tucked away.

In 1933 Sir Alfred anonymously sold fifteen Brontë paintings and drawings, and several manuscripts at a Hodgson & Co. auction. Of the items sold, several have since

Top left: an unfinished drawing by Anne Brontë of her dog Flossy. Flossy was given to Anne by her pupils whilst working as a governess with the Robinson family at Thorp Green. She outlived Anne by a number of years, eventually dying in December 1854. The drawing was included in the 1933 Hodgson & Co. auction of Law items, and bought by the Brontë Society.

Top right: oil painting by Branwell Brontë of Jacob's dream taken from the book of Genesis. The painting was donated to the Museum in 1894 by William Law.

Left: pencil drawing by Emily Brontë of a young woman in a tiara dated October 6th 1841. This was bought by William Law from Tabitha Ratcliffe, younger sister of Martha Brown. It was then included in the 1933 sale at Hodgson & Co. and was later donated to the Museum by J. Roy Coventry.

These three tiny drawings, formerly part of the Law collection, were bought at auction in 2004. They were produced by Charlotte Bronte, with the exception of the sketch of a woman and parrot, which has been attributed to Branwell.

found their way into the Museum collection. He is said to have parted with the remaining manuscripts to a mysterious London bookseller around this time, but there has never been any evidence to prove this was the case.

Sir Alfred Law also gave some of the collection to his nurse. These items were considered of lesser importance by Law, but nevertheless included: a chalk portrait of Charlotte Brontë, a flintlock pistol – probably that described by Emily in *Wuthering Heights* – miniature sketches by Charlotte and Branwell, Emily's artist's box and geometry set, her spectacles and a selection of books owned by the family. Charlotte's desk and Emily's artist's box and geometry set were auctioned in 2009, and the other items in 2004. Sadly the Museum was unable to purchase the desk, but the successful bidder kindly donated it to the Museum shortly afterwards. The Brontë Society managed to secure a number of other lots, however, and they are now at Haworth.

Today we have Davidson Cook's transcript of the Law Brontë archive, but the whereabouts of most of his valuable collection is still a mystery.

The Monthly Intelligencer

[F]rom March 27. AD 1833. To April. 26 th. Justice Great. Glass Town P Bronte. M

A Few words To The Chief Geni;

[W]hen a Parent leaves his=
[c]hildern young and inexper
[i]ences. and without a cause
[a]bsconds. never more troub
[l]ing himself about them
[t]hose Childern according to
[r]eceived notions among men
[i]f they by good Fortune –
[s]hould happen to survive
[h]is neglect and beome of –
[r]epute in society are by
[n]o means bound. to believe
[t]hat he has done ~~their~~ his
[d]uty to them as a parent.
[m]erely because they have.
[r]isen. nor are They indeed
[r]equired to own or Treat
[h]im as a parent. This is all
[v]ery plain. and we believe
[t]hat for our readers will
[u]nderstand our aim in thus
speaking

A child of the G–i

A VISIT TO Elvington Hall : by A.B.C

[O]ne day last week. I received
[a]n invitation to a grand dinn
[e]r which was to be given by Alex
[a]nder Rougue. Viscount Elvin
[g]ton! on the occasion of his
[r]ecent marriage on the app
[o]inted evening my carriage
[d]rew up in Front of his –
[r]egal. Mansion on stepping
[o]ut I was ushered. immed
[i]ately into the Great Hall a
[m]ost noble apartment blaz
[i]ng with light and hung –
with gold and velvet. every
[t]hing around me was cond
[u]cted upon such a scale a
[n]othing but the most prin
[c]ly fortune could keep up
[u]pon my entrance I found
[t]hat as yet but few of the
[c]ompany had arrived neve[r]
[a]nd our Host and Hostess=
[m]ade their appearance the
First Person whom I rec
[o]gnised was little Charlie
[W]ellesly squatted under a
[c]hair and playing with a
[h]uge dog not being able
[t]o extract any rational from
him I passed on to where
stood my old friend Capt
Bud. his hands in his pock
[e]ts and his eyes now cast
[s]orrowfully upon his fair
[r]ound paunch and now
[w]andering surveying every
door in expectation of the
[l]ong delayed. dinner havin[g]
[e]ntered in to conversation

as the Thrice celebrated –
John Gifford. at the soun[d]
of this name a hideous
army of dusty and cobw
ebs ponderous Tomes &
rusty armour. attacked –
my defenceless imaginat
ion I decamped leaving
them both engaged in
a profound disscussion up
on the blade of a Roman
Knife which had been
lately dug up in Buds =
garden and which when
I left them he was jus[t]
hauling from his pocket
for a more rigid scrutiny
However before I had
proceeded many yards a
most deathlike groan from
Gifford. announced some
dreadful discovery I turned
round and beheld. Bud stan
ding with eyes and arms up
lifted in unutterable morti
fication. While Gifford was
reading "as if were his neck
verse" the word marked
upon the rusty blade =
"Swashing Tom, Cutler G G
Town 1823." leaving this
distracted pair I steer
ed immediatly toward the
Principle table where we[re]
standing divers groups o vis
itors admiring the various
and costly works of art
under which it groaned –
before one party lay spre[a]d
the magnificent nay glor
ious work De Lisles ~~Glass~~
~~Town dele~~ "Verdopolitan del
ineata" a vast Elephant.
Folio of perhaps the most
splendid engraving of the
most splendid Architecture
which ever existed. others
were examing the 5 quarto
of Dundees Scenery of the
Glass Town countrys other
a profusion of the most
richly bound richly eng
raven and costly works wi[t]
h could be conceived.
Apart from these and
far retired stood the =
two men of Millions Buck
ingham and Grenville deb
ating together upon the
affairs of Empires and
bargaining away the wealth
of Ages Joyous bursts of
laughter now allowed
me to the Fireplace =
round which were ~~stand~~
~~ing~~ gathered young Lofty
The Elvingtons and a whole
host of the sprouts of the
spirits of the Glass Town
boasting and telling feats
of their dogs horses char
iots and themselves. The

with the Marquis and
Marchioness of Douro all
eyes were turned toward
them. and truly it puzzl
ed one to judge which
of the four in appearance
held the preference the
contrast to was so strik
ing between them. Rougue
advanced tall and stately.
with a stern aristocratic
expressio upon a countenance
ance which though shatter
ed and worn with late and
dissipation. yet presented
an expression astonishingly
noble and intellectual. mix
ed it is true with somethi
ng so secret cold and sarc
astic that the spectator felt
~~only~~ on beholding an invol
untary awe and creeping of the
flesh. ~~The~~ Marquis on the
contrary entered the room
with a cheerful though =
noble aspect his bright eyes
beaming with and congratulat
ion. to all around him and
his ~~+~~ firm an upright figu
re presenting all the str
ength and vigour of a joy
ous and unharrased youth.
Betwen Lady Zenobia and
the Marchioness of Douro
their existed as striking
a contrast the one so high
and haughty ...
so freezingly exclusive the
other so young gay and =
merry that the the humbl
est and poorest being on
earth would ~~[illegible]~~ feel delight
and confidence when speak
ing to her. of the beauty of
either it is needless to =
speak. Company now beg
an to flow fast in a great
rattleing carriages was heard
at the door then a great
bustle in the hall and soon
the door being flung open
their entered followed by
a train of attendants 4 men
of the old days tall stern.
built as if of iron with =
frank yet peirceing aspect
and ornamented with many
scars ~~and~~ on their lofty =
forheads every one stood
up and bowed ~~to [illegible]~~
with the greatest reverence
to these the FOUR KINGS
OF ASHANTEE Sneaky Welling
ton Parry and Ross dinner
was now announced and
~~were~~ we were all ushered
into the dining hall a room
still more spacious and =
splendid than the ~~th~~ one
we had left it was the
summum bonum of mag
nificence. ~~[illegible]~~ of the
dinner it is sufficient
to say that it comprised all

ever been seen ...
dinner being no...
the ladies ~~witho~~...
~~vam um had~~ ...
younger and m...
ous gentlemen ...
to the sitting ro...
rum uns and ...
drawn the chai...
the fire and w...
in disscusing ...
comfort of life ...
justice was do...
qualitys and ...
bottle disappear...
such vast rapid...
Feared we sho...
new edition o...
eme's science ...
upon his thron...
of the feast se...
example to ev...
emptying with ...
perfect steady...
steadyness of ...
steadyness of h...
glass after g...
lle down his w...
masters – tried ...
king. ~~[illegible]~~ ...
elevated ...
the ladies and ...
their childer...
st of this joyo...
captain ...
ily engaged in ...
cut of somme...
from his sea...
the table and ...
caper near th...
high uttered s...
ing scream th...
this soul was ...
clay. he continu...
about in convuls...
fright and ago...
Oh my leg my ...
all for amom...
were in const...
at the strange ...
till a shrill ...
laugh from u...
table unravelled ...
mystery and ...
~~the~~ young Charl...
ing an immen...
his hand. and ...
peals of eldri...
ran up to to ...
when he esp...
became ~~[illegible]~~ ...
ilicontrollable. ...
about in ever...
pursued by th...
rougue. at this ...
we all burst ...
a ~~[illegible]~~ of lau...
~~[illegible]~~ while Rou...
ing from his ...
after. great a...

You will please return these when you have done with them – Don't let Mr Wise appropriate them.

Arthur Bell Nicholls, in a letter to Clement Shorter, 1895

Photograph of Thomas J. Wise.

THOMAS J. WISE

THROUGHOUT 1895 A steady stream of Brontë letters and manuscripts was sent by Arthur Bell Nicholls to the writer Clement Shorter to help him write his planned biography of Charlotte. At first he trusted to Shorter's discretion not to publish any details that might reflect badly on Charlotte. In 1896, though, he was growing wary, and sent eight letters with the accompanying note: "You will please return these when you have done with them – Don't let Mr Wise appropriate them".

His plea was too late. Shorter had already passed on the bulk of the Brontë manuscripts to his associate Thomas J. Wise, then a well-known scholar and bibliophile with a fast-growing reputation, who had paid around £400 for them.

It would be 35 years before Wise was exposed as a conman: one of history's most prolific literary forgers, responsible for decades of confusion among Brontë scholars.

Thomas J. Wise was born into a working-class family in Gravesend, Kent, in 1859, son of a tobacconist. As a boy he frequented London's Farringdon Road, buying up second-hand books from barrows. Slowly he learned to tell the difference between those worth selling on, and those good only for scrap. His purchases of valuable editions of Thomas Moore's *Epicurean* and Shelley's *Cenci* convinced him he should

Clement Shorter, who obtained Brontë manuscripts and letters on behalf of Wise.

Opposite page: *The Monthly Intelligencer*, a miniature newspaper produced by Branwell between 27 March and 26 April 1833.

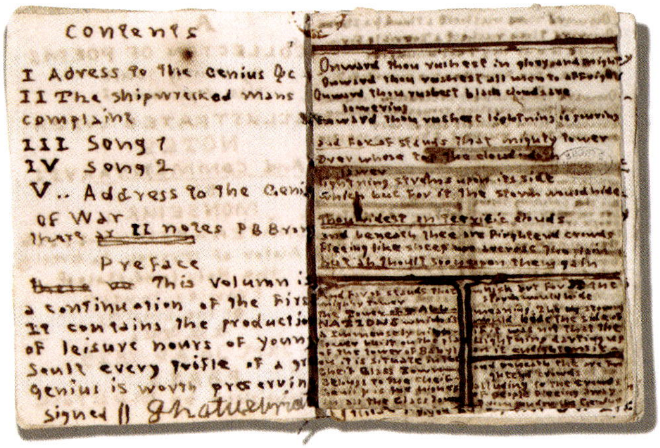

Above: *A Collection of Poems by Young Soult*, a 'little book' produced by Branwell in 1829.

Left: Branwell's *Battell Book* is one of the earliest surviving Brontë manuscripts. It was acquired by Wise and purchased by the Brontë Society from his agent, Herbert Gorfin.

dedicate his life to collecting, and these two books formed the basis of his grandly-titled collection, 'The Ashley Library', named after his address at the time, 52 Ashley Road, Hornsey Rise, north London.

The library rapidly expanded, and in 1895 Wise's wife Selina Fanny deserted him on the grounds that he was more devoted to his books than to their marriage. He quickly found another wife, however, and Louise was soon as dedicated to the Ashley Library as was her husband.

Wise began his working life as a cashier at essential oil merchant Rubeck's on Mark Lane in the City of London. At work he sold oils to soap and perfume manufacturers; at home he began writing to every famous author and budding literary society in the hope of obtaining more rare manuscripts for his library. When these proved hard to come by he began to print his own.

Taking early editions of famous works such as Elizabeth Barrett Browning's *Sonnets From the Portuguese*, or John Ruskin's *Leoni; A Legend of Italy*, Wise would copy and rebind them, then claim them to be 'pre-first' editions, privately printed for circulation among the author's friends, and thus highly valuable. Slowly he would release these copies on to the market, often donating a few to libraries or literary societies in an attempt to establish himself as a serious book collector and philanthropist. In one case he even managed to get the author William Morris to autograph a forgery of his own poem *Sir Galahad*.

All the time he was reinforcing his reputation as a serious scholar and collector. 'Bibliography appeals to me in the strongest possible manner,' he wrote to the collector John H. Wrenn. 'I would never stand in the way to hinder its progress for the sake of satisfying my selfish ends.'

By June 1895 he was in possession of 25 of the Brontë children's 'little books', as well as a large collection of Charlotte's letters, and some manuscripts of Branwell's. Cashing in on the booming interest in Brontë memorabilia, he cut up pages and had them rebound for lucrative sales to the American market. Branwell's work he passed off as being by Charlotte, in order to fetch higher prices.

Wise was eventually elected Brontë Society President, and published a knowledgeable index, *Bibliography of the Works of All Members of the Brontë Family and of Brontëana*, which, of course, authenticated his own forgeries. President of the Bibliographical Society and honorary fellow of Worcester College, Oxford, he rode high on his reputation. Then in 1934 he was unmasked by the scholars John Carter and Graham Pollard.

Carter and Pollard had been suspicious for a long time that none of these 'pre-first' editions were inscribed, and all were bound so similarly. With long and patient detective work they established them as forgeries, and published their findings.

Three years later Wise was dead, his reputation in tatters. The slow work of retrieving and piecing together the Brontës' manuscripts and letters now began in earnest, but for decades there were still gaps – many literal – in our understanding of the Brontës' work. Sadly, many of these gaps still exist.

The Brontës' cabinet piano was included in the sale, held at the Parsonage in 1861. It passed through several hands before being put up for sale at Sotheby's as part of the Dixon collection.

In the sale rooms wealthy collectors could always outbid the Society, and this often meant that not only Haworth, but England, lost the literary treasures that belonged to her, so more and more people sent their Brontë souvenirs to Haworth as gifts.

Edith Weir, *Brontë Parsonage Museum Guidebook*, 1962

The Story Continues

A watercolour by Branwell entitled *Praise*, and dated 9 September 1830. Purchased in 1998.

Given the history of their dispersal, it is incredible that so many of the Brontës' manuscripts, letters and personal possessions have returned to their original home at Haworth. Although there are many Brontë items in overseas collections, the largest collection is held at the Brontë Parsonage Museum.

Other prominent collectors of Brontëana included J. H. Dixon of Harrogate. Dixon amassed a large collection, much of it acquired through Haworth sources, which was displayed at his home, Oatlands House in Harrogate. Following his death the collection was put up for sale at Sotheby's in 1916. Some lots were withdrawn from the sale and presented to the Brontë Museum by the Dixon family; one item acquired through this source was the Brontës' cabinet piano.

J. Roy Coventry of Liverpool also found Haworth a rich source of Brontëana. On a single visit in August 1907 he purchased a number of items from Mrs Ratcliffe, including a letter by Patrick Brontë, Branwell's pencil drawing of a cat, the tiny stool used by Emily, and a bundle of letters sent to her sister Martha from Arthur Bell Nicholls. At the time of his death in 1942 Coventry's collection returned to Haworth as a bequest.

Several Brontë biographers also became collectors. One of these is Mrs Ellis Chadwick, who spent the first two years of her married life living in Haworth. Although her biography, *In the Footsteps of the Brontës*, was not published until 1914, much of the research had been carried out during her time in Haworth in the late 1880s, when several of those associated with the family were still alive. As well as gathering

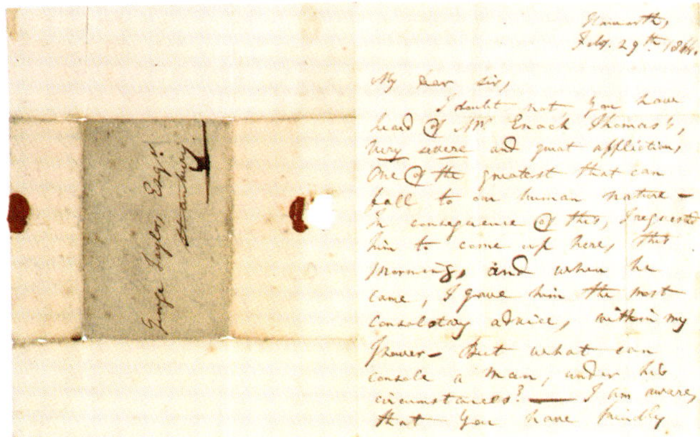

George Taylor, Esqr.
Stanbury

Haworth,
Feby. 29th 1844.

My dear Sir,
I doubt not you have heard of Mr Enoch Thomas's, very severe and great affliction, one of the greatest that can fall to our human nature — in consequence of this, I requested him to come up here, this morning, and when he came, I gave him the most consolatory advice, within my power — But what can console a man, under his circumstances? — I am aware, that you have kindly

Left: a portrait in oils of Maria Taylor by Branwell. Purchased by the Brontë Society in 2007 with support from the MLA/V&A Purchase Grant Fund and The Art Fund.

Right: Patrick Brontë letter to George Taylor of Stanbury, 29 February 1844. Purchased by the Brontë Society at Christie's in 2007.

information, Mrs Chadwick also acquired a collection of Brontë items. These included a dress and Spanish lace veil worn by Charlotte, along with other costume items and original letters, mainly purchased from Martha Brown's nieces Mary E. Popplewell and Eleanor Scarborough. Mrs Chadwick died in 1929 and was buried in Haworth. Her Brontë collection was sold at Sotheby's in 1947, and most lots were purchased by the Brontë Society.

Daphne du Maurier, probably best known for her novel *Rebecca* (1938), made her first visit to Haworth in 1954 while working on a preface to a new edition of *Wuthering Heights*. The Brontës, with their Cornish ancestry, held a strong appeal for du Maurier, which developed into a fascination with the ill-fated Branwell. Although best known as a novelist, Daphne du Maurier was the author of several biographies, and her biography of Branwell, *The Infernal World of Branwell Brontë*, was published in 1960. The book was the culmination of much thorough research, during which she was inspired to purchase several original manuscripts by Branwell from the library of J. A. Symington, who had greatly encouraged her, and to whom the biography was dedicated. Daphne du Maurier became a life member of the Brontë Society, and in 1961 donated five of her Branwell manuscripts to the Brontë Parsonage Museum.

Over the years the Brontë Society's collection has continued to grow. In 2009 several important Brontë items were donated by Tony Hart of Manitoba, Canada, whose great-grandfather was the nephew of Mary Bell, the second wife of Arthur Bell Nicholls. The collection included a fragmentary manuscript by Charlotte dated 1829, entitled

Left: Emily's artist's box and geometry set, which became part of the Law collection, and were purchased by the Brontë Society at Sotheby's in 2009.

Right: a portrait of Zenobia, Marchioness Ellrington by Charlotte, 15 October 1833. Purchased from a private owner in 2009 with support from the MLA/V&A Purchase Grant Fund and The Art Fund.

Anecdotes of the Duke of Wellington, and an accompanying drawing of a Wellington monument. A mahogany writing desk once used by Charlotte Brontë, and formerly part of the Law collection, was sold at Sotheby's in the same year, and donated to the Museum by its new owner.

Other recent donations have included Anne Brontë's workbox, with its original contents. This had passed to Martha Brown's sister Tabitha Ratcliffe, and was donated by one of her descendants. There are many more Brontë items in private ownership. Some of these are known from descriptions in sale catalogues, letters and contemporary accounts. Many more wait to be rediscovered.

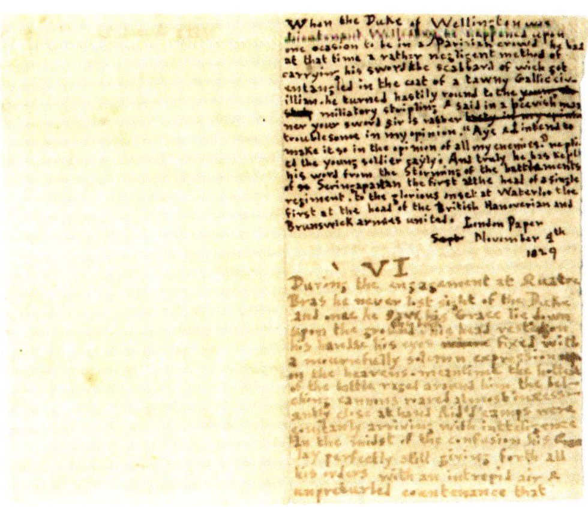

When the Duke of Wellington was
Lieutenant Wellesley he happened upon
one ocasion to be in a Parisian crowd he had
at that time a rather negligent method of
carrying his sword the scabbard of wich got
entangled in the coat of a tawny Gallic civ-
illian. he turned hastily round to the [illegible]
[illegible] militory stripling & said in a peevish [illegible]
ner your sword sir is rather [illegible]
troublesome in my opinion." "Aye and intend to
make it so in the opinion of all my enemies." repli-
ed the young soldier gayly. And truly he has kept
his word from the Storming of the battlements
of Seringapatam the first at the head of a single
regiment. to the glorious onset at Waterloo the
first at the head of the British Hanoverian and
Brunswick armies united. London Paper
Sept November 4th
1829

VI

During the engagement at [illegible]
was he never lost sight of the Duke
and once he gave his horse lie down
upon the ground his head resting on
his hands his eyes fixed with
a wonderfully solemn expression
on the heavens [illegible]
of the battle raged around him the bel-
ching cannons roared almost incess-
antly close at hand Aid-de-camps were
constantly arriving with intelligence
In the midst of the confusion his Grace
lay perfectly still giving forth all
his orders with an intrepid air &
unperturbed countenance that

Above: a tiny drawing of a Wellington monument by Charlotte, forming one of the pages of her manuscript *Anecdotes of the Duke of Wellington* and dated January 1831.

Left: *Anecdotes of the Duke of Wellington* by Charlotte, 1829. Part of a collection of items donated by Tony Hart in 2009.

Bronte - to W.S. Williams Esq
65 Cornhill
London

Jane Eyre - Shirley - Villette -

13

76 2

BEAUTIF
PERFEC
PERMAN

My dear Sir

I have at last got my parcel which I find consists not only of newspapers but of books — you really are — all of you — too good.

I took up one of the books directly: its title attracted me — Lady Morgan's "Woman & her Master" of course I have as yet perused but little of it — too little, perhaps, to warrant me in declaring an opinion — but I will tell you how I am impressed, candidly — not favourably. Not content with elevating "woman", she seeks to degrade "Man" — this is not fair. Moreover her style is very pompous; she prefers long, sounding words to short, simple ones: then too, one feels that she often writes rather from a

[TH]E LIFE AND WORKS OF CHARLO[TTE] BRONTE AND HER SISTERS.

[...] introduction by Mrs. Humphry Ward an[d ...]ons. Jane Eyre, Vol. I., Haworth [...] [Sm]ith, Elder, and Co.).

[...]ass judgment upon the latest edition of Ja[ne ...] be to criticise a critic, and one who is bet[ter ...]ourselves to pronounce sentence, for no o[ne ...]ntly fitted to adjudge the merits of the [...]tte Bronte as a woman who has herself m[...]fficulties and felt the secret delight of pour[...]ter with a pen. Messrs. Smith, Elder, a[nd ...]cored a success in inviting Mrs. Humphry [...]to an introduction to their new issue of Jan[e ...]opularity belongs to the past rather th[...]t. The excitement that provoked the au[...]ty Fair" to jealousy after ten years of w[...]as died away. The Charlotte Bronte [...] and od-fashioned, and though only fifty yea[rs ...] since its first publication, it is in close[...]he days of Addison rather than with ou[...] as much is to praise rather than conden[...] who want literature in colour rather than [...]my shadows will still find a rare and in[...] of description in Jane Eyre. Mrs. Wa[rd ...] appreciate the magic vitality which [...]h the veins of this work. She [...]here was never a plot of looser texture, or [...]f inconsistencies and absurdities: but t[...]onality—a strong, free, passionate perso[...] is the sole but sufficient spell of [...] Charlotte Bronte's individuality w[...] several causes, to her parenta[...]er greed of reading. Mrs. [...]:—"As to the Celtic pride, the [...]s, the Celtic endurance, Charlotte Bronte v[...]m all. Her nature loves to give—recoil[...] in society she will neither be exhibi[...]sed." Was it not natural that the daug[hter ...]hman in county Down, and of a Cornish [...] display all these nervous characteristic[s ...]s also indebted to her love of French literat[ure ...] is constantly something in her mode of ap[...] subject, even in the turn of the sentence[...]n the use of participles which is French [...]nglish." In allowing this we have to bear [...] was the day of Victor Hugo, Musset, and

November 1899

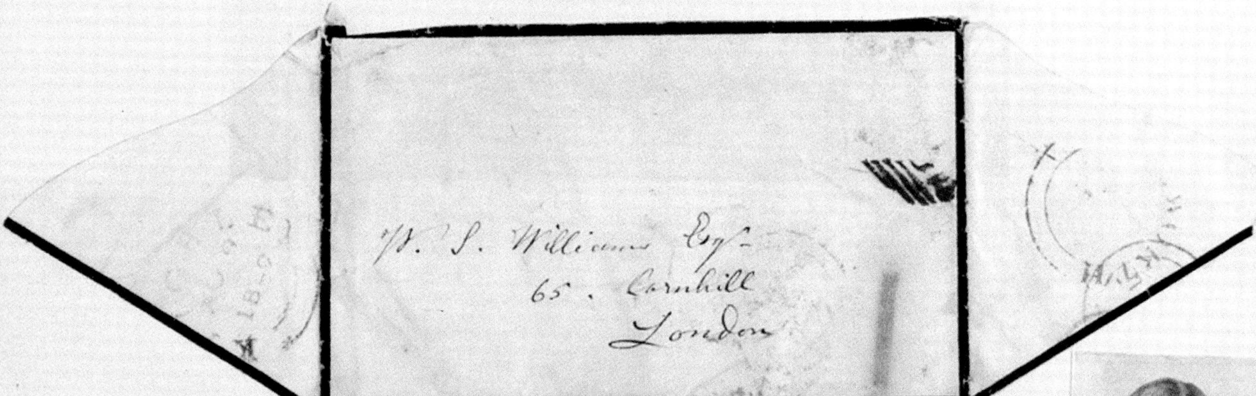

Charlotte Brontë.

Further Reading

Christine Alexander & Jane Sellars
The Art of the Brontës
Cambridge University Press, 1995

H. K. Bell
'Charlotte Brontë's husband: his later life and surroundings'
The Cornhill Magazine, January, 1927

Henry H. Bonnell
Charlotte Brontë, George Eliot and Jane Austen: Studies in their Works
Longmans, Green and Co., 1902

John Carter and Graham Pollard
An Enquiry into the Nature of Certain Nineteenth Century Pamphlets
Constable, 1934

Davidson Cook
'Brontë Manuscripts in the Law Collection'
The Bookman, November, 1925

Ann Dinsdale
The Brontës at Haworth
Frances Lincoln, 2006

Jennifer Glynn
Prince of Publishers: A Biography of the Great Victorian Publisher George Smith
Allison and Busby, 1986

Charles Lemon
Early Visitors to Haworth: from Ellen Nussey to Virginia Woolf
The Brontë Society, 1996

Opposite page: a Charlotte Brontë letter to W. S. Williams and accompanying envelope, mounted on a page taken from an album. Purchased by the Brontë Society at Christie's in 2007.

Wilfred Partington
Thomas J. Wise in the Original Cloth: The Life and Record of the Forger of the Nineteenth-Century Pamphlets
Robert Hale, 1946

Fannie E. Ratchford
Letters of Thomas Wise to John Henry Wrenn: A Further Enquiry Into the Guilt of Certain Nineteenth-Century Forgers
Alfred A. Knopf, 1944

Clement K. Shorter, ed.
The Four Wishes: A Fairy Tale by Charlotte Brontë
Privately printed, 1918

John Smurthwaite
The Life of John Alexander Symington, Bibliographer and Librarian, 1887-1961: A Bookman's Rise and Fall
The Edwin Mellen Press, 1995

Kathleen Tillotson
'Back to the beginning of this century'
Brontë Society Transactions: 19.1&2.3, 1986

Barbara Whitehead
Charlotte Brontë and her 'dearest Nell': The story of a friendship
Smith Settle, 1993

Stephen Whitehead
'Henry Bonnell: guardian of the relics of passion'
Brontë Studies: 30.1.31, 2005

Tom Winnifrith
The Brontës and Their Background: Romance and Reality
The Macmillan Press, 1973

The Brontë Society

Founded in 1893, the Brontë Society is one of the oldest literary societies in the world, and its membership today is one of the largest and most active. The Society promotes academic research into the Brontës' lives and works, and sponsors a wide range of education programmes. The Society also owns and manages the Brontë family's home, Haworth Parsonage, now the Brontë Parsonage Museum, which houses the world's largest collection of Brontë manuscripts, paintings, personal effects and memorabilia. As a registered charity, the Society is managed by a Board of Trustees elected by its members. Membership of the Society therefore confers direct, democratic influence on the management of the Museum and the Society's collection.

Other benefits of Brontë Society membership include:

- Free admission to the Brontë Parsonage Museum
- Free entry to the Museum for up to three accompanied children up to the age of 16
- A starter pack with membership card
- Free issues of the Society's *Gazette*
- June members' weekend including Church Service, Annual General Meeting, address by an eminent speaker, day excursions and social events
- An annual Literary Lunch and Spring Walk.

If you are interested in becoming a member of the Brontë Society, please contact the Society Administrator at:

The Brontë Parsonage Museum,
Haworth, Keighley, West Yorkshire BD22 8DR

Telephone : +44 (0) 1535 640195

Fax +44 (0) 1535 647131

Email: membership@bronte.org.uk

Website: www.bronte.info